PRINCESITA

COLORING BOOK

Sabat Beatto

Princess Coloring Book

Can you color my dress?

Add color to your royal princess!

Coloring Book:

Coloring book for kids and adults.

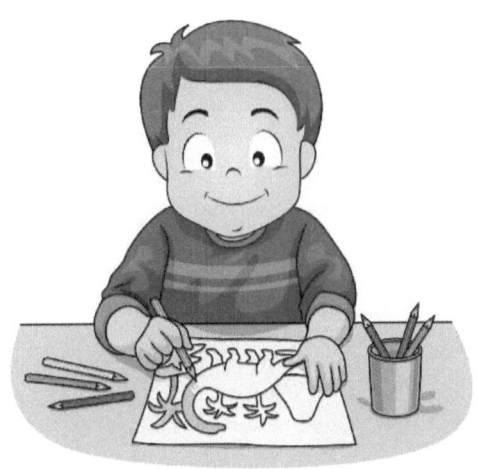

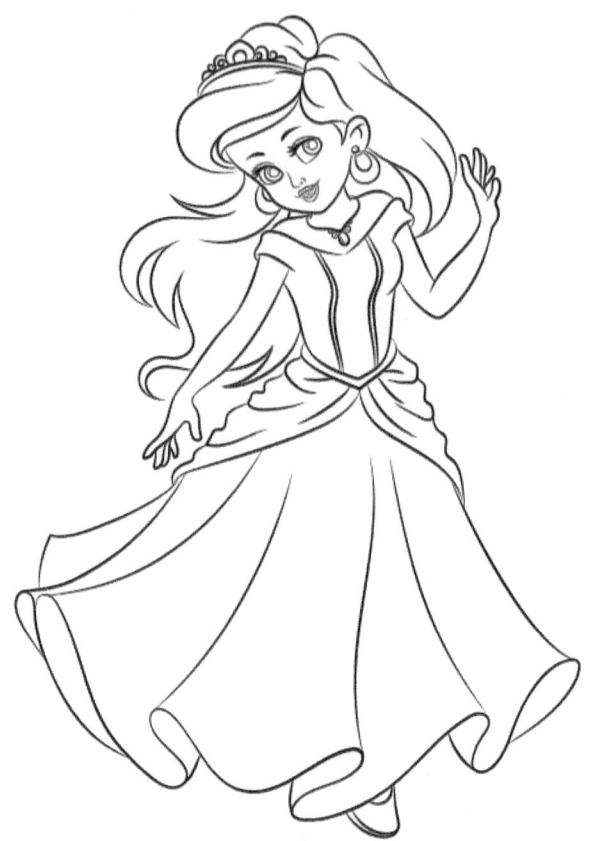

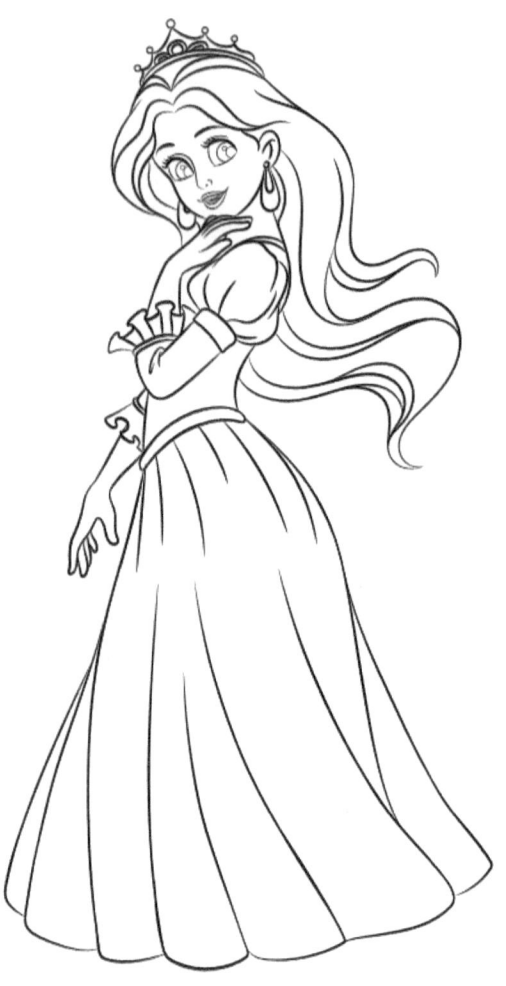

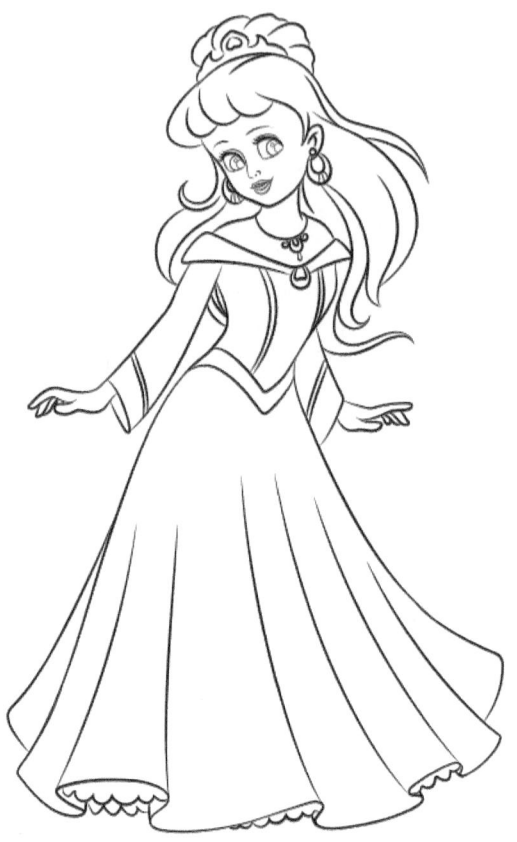

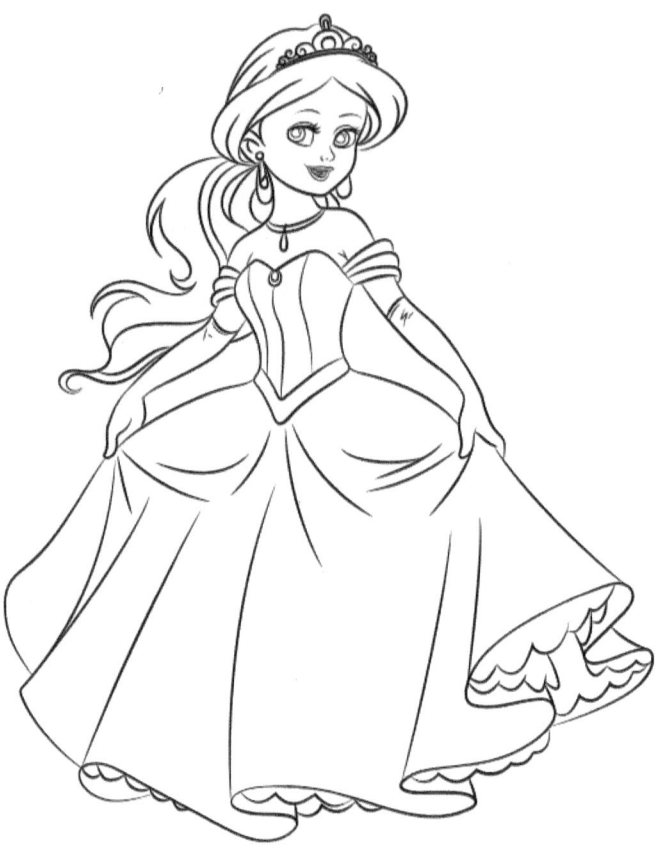

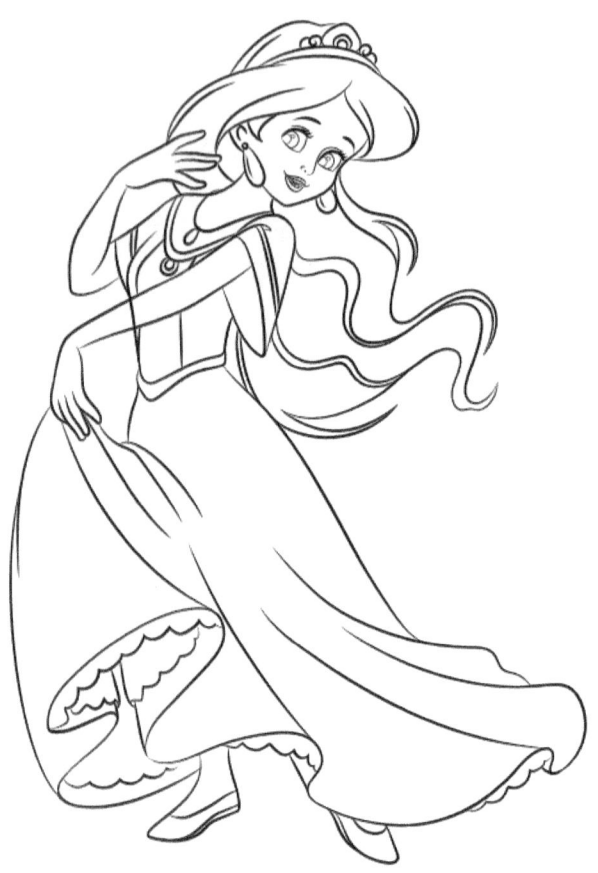

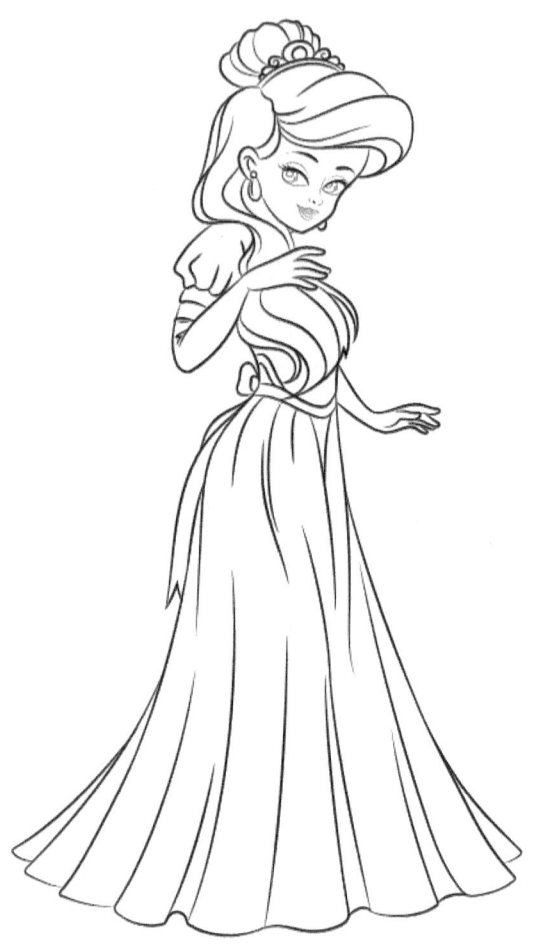

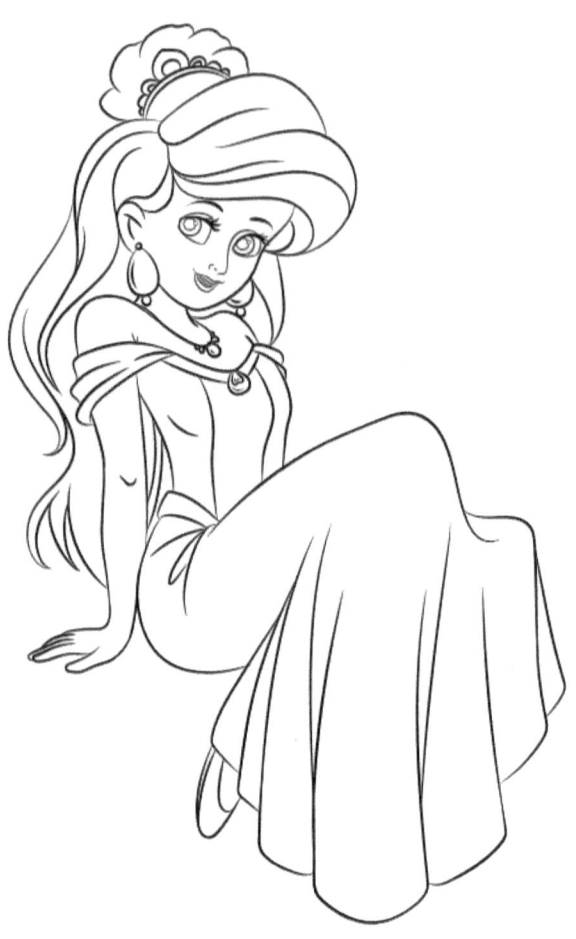

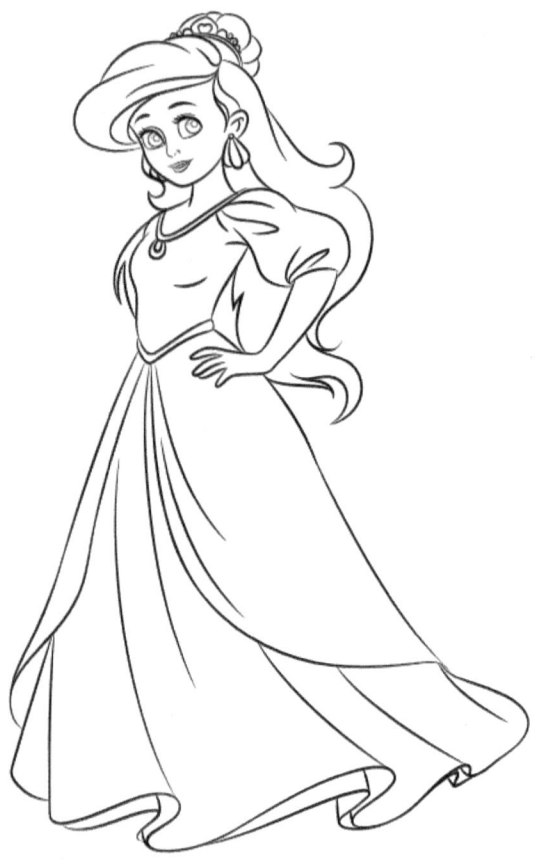

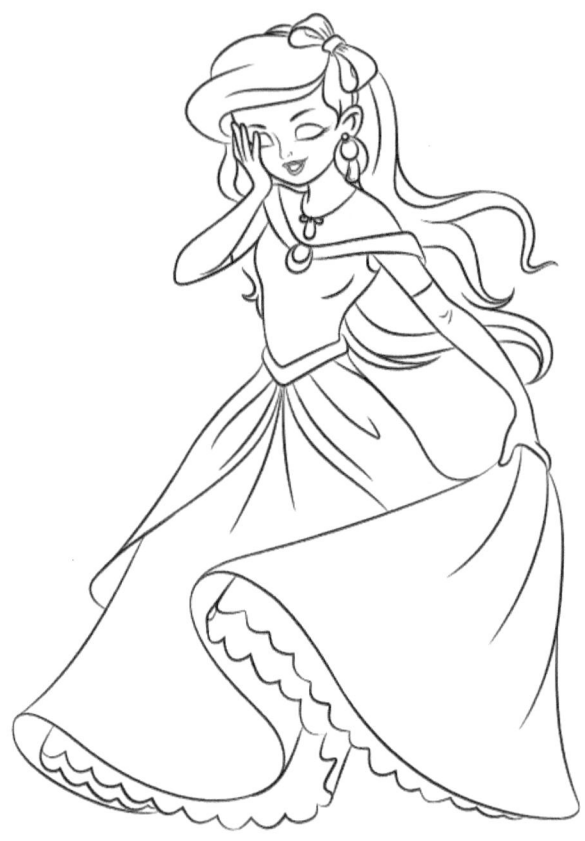

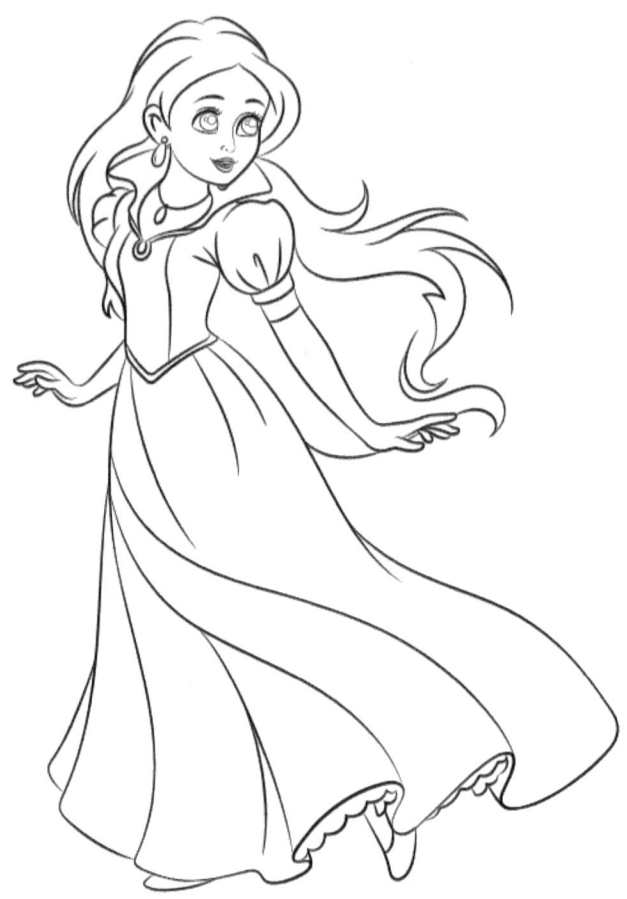

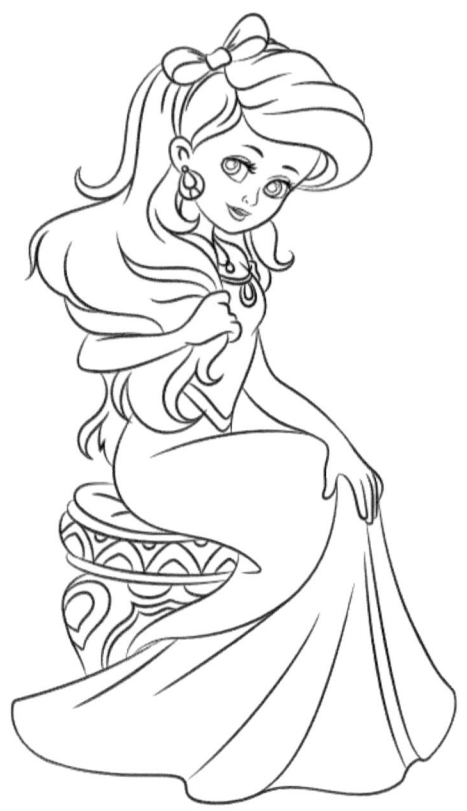

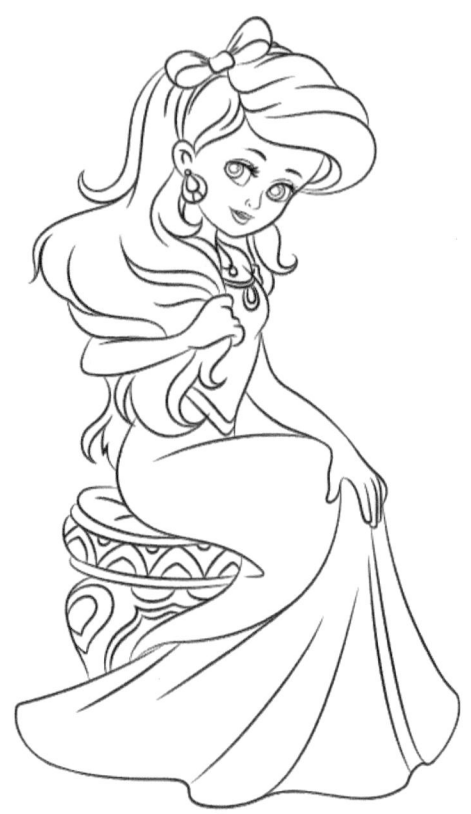

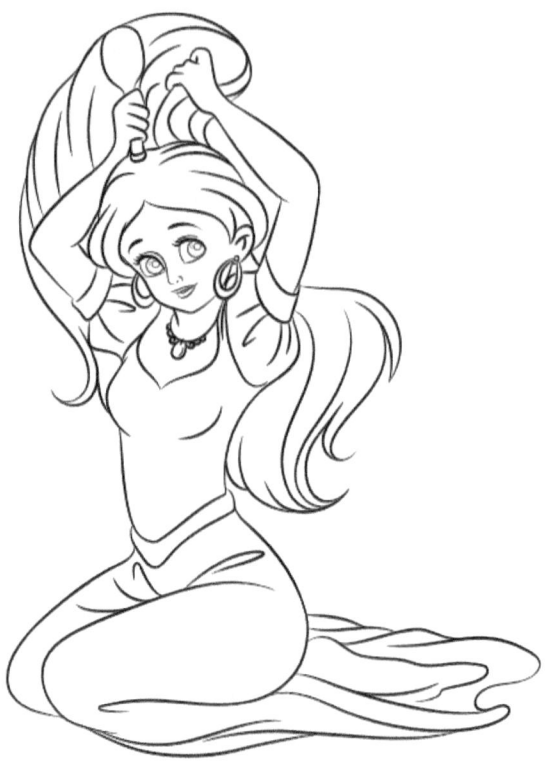

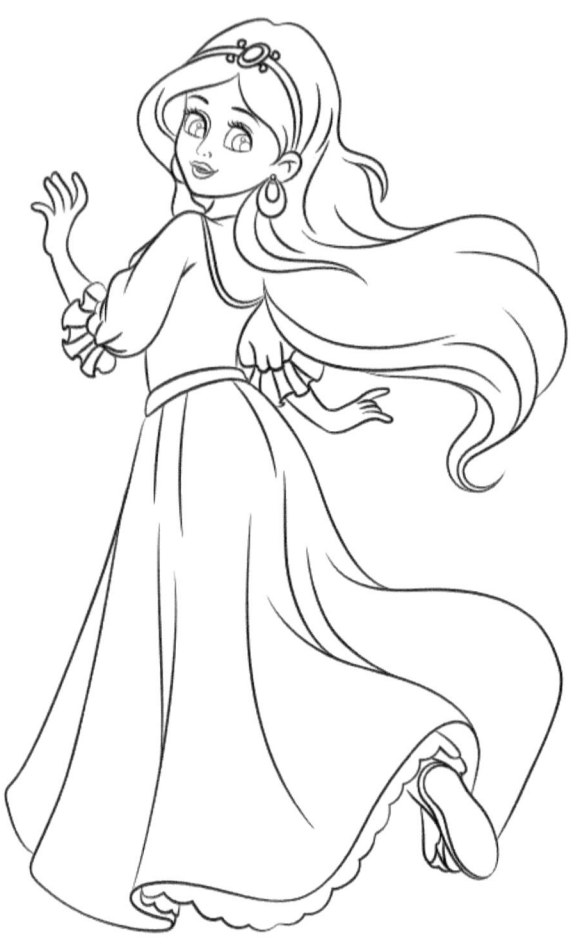

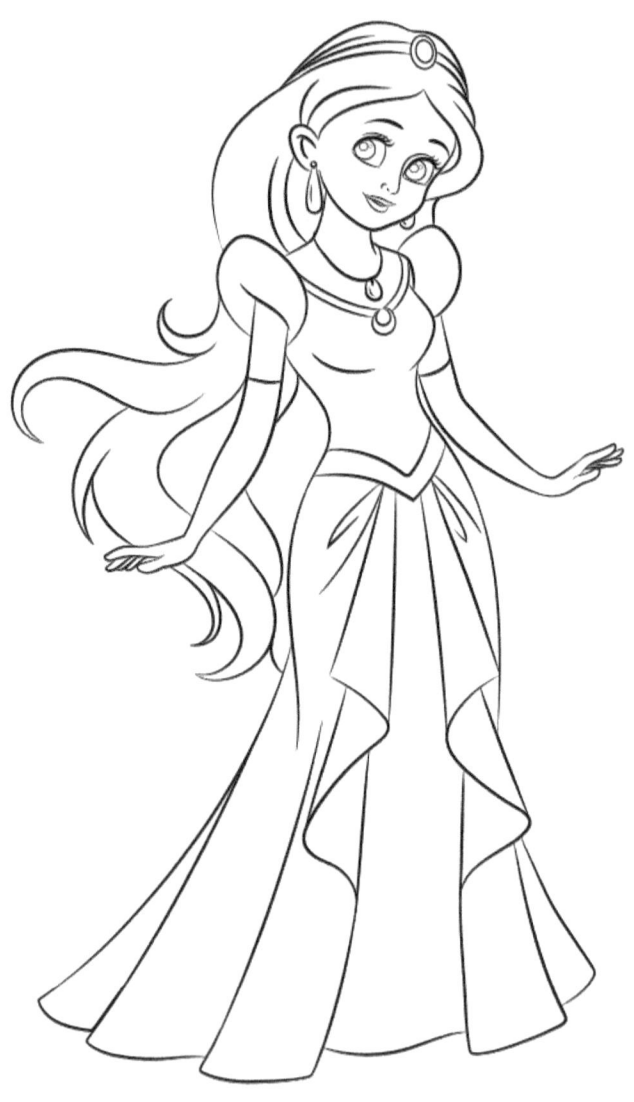

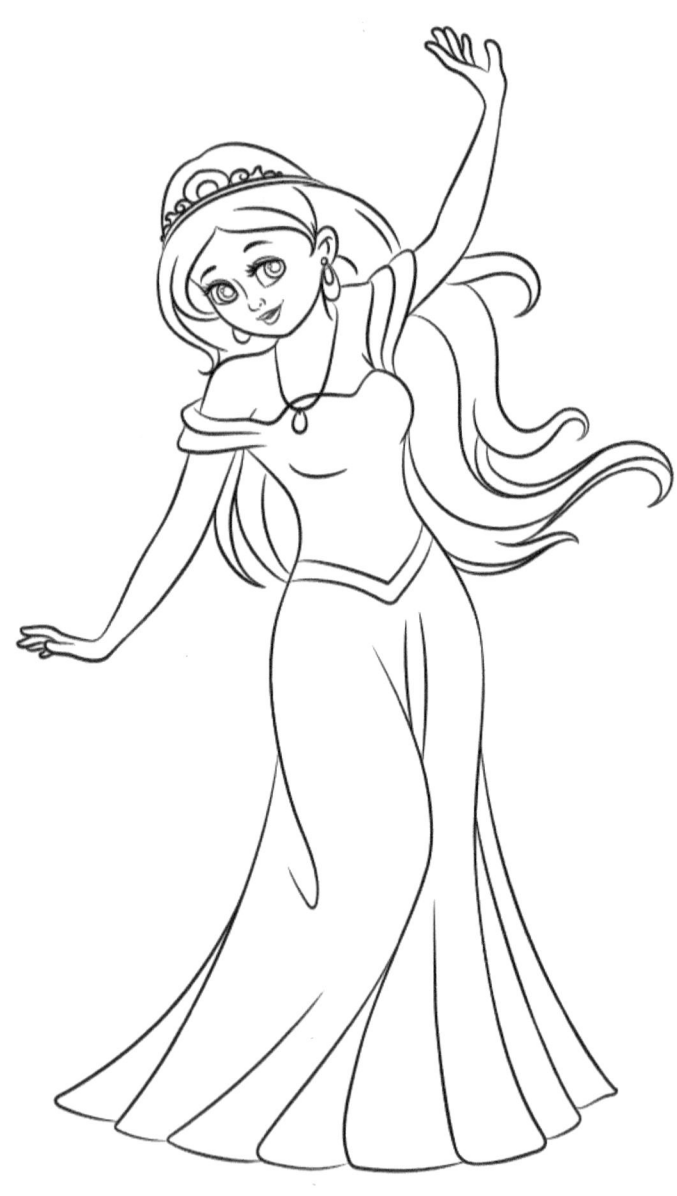

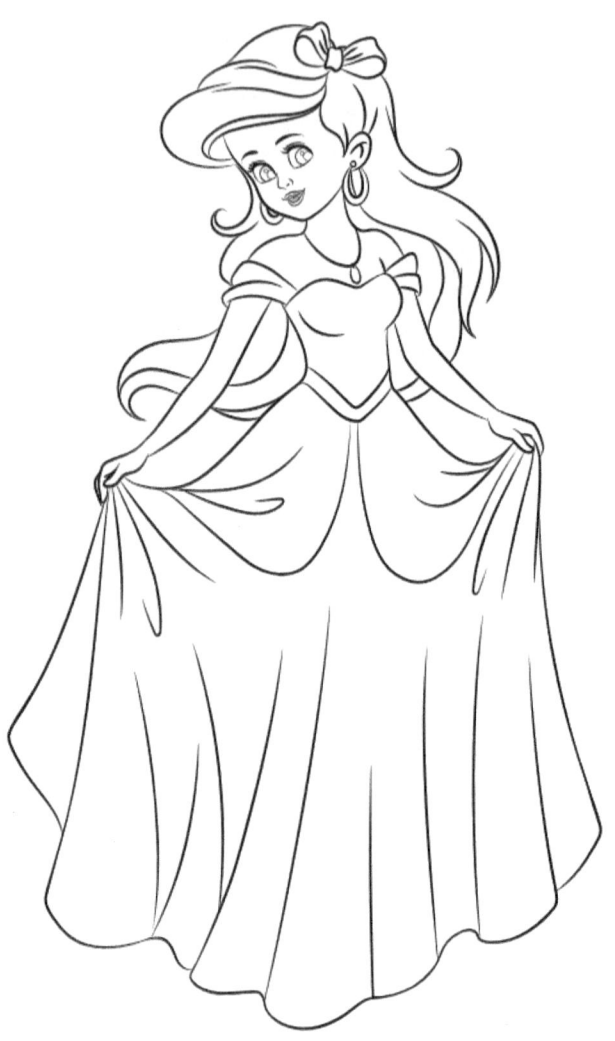

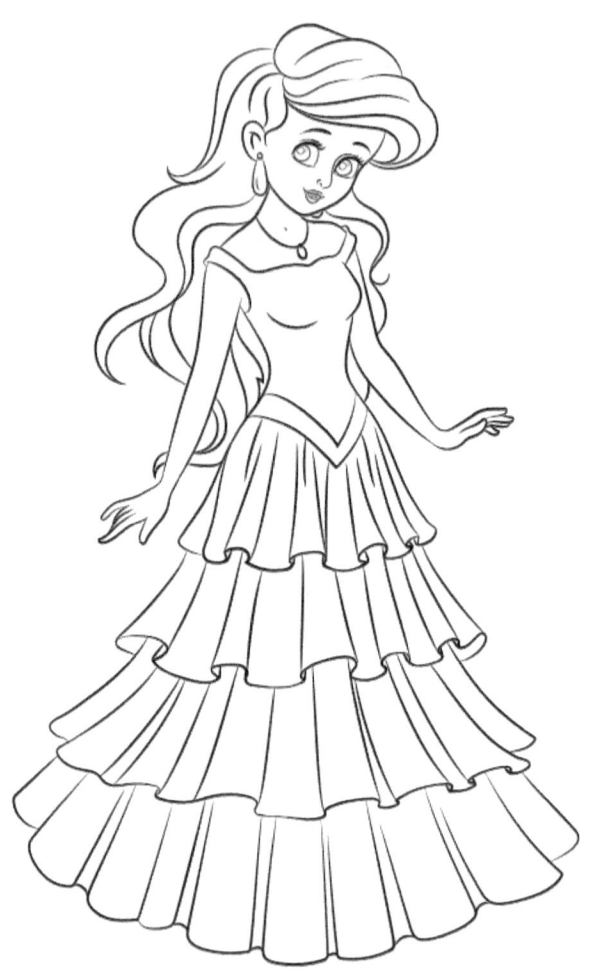

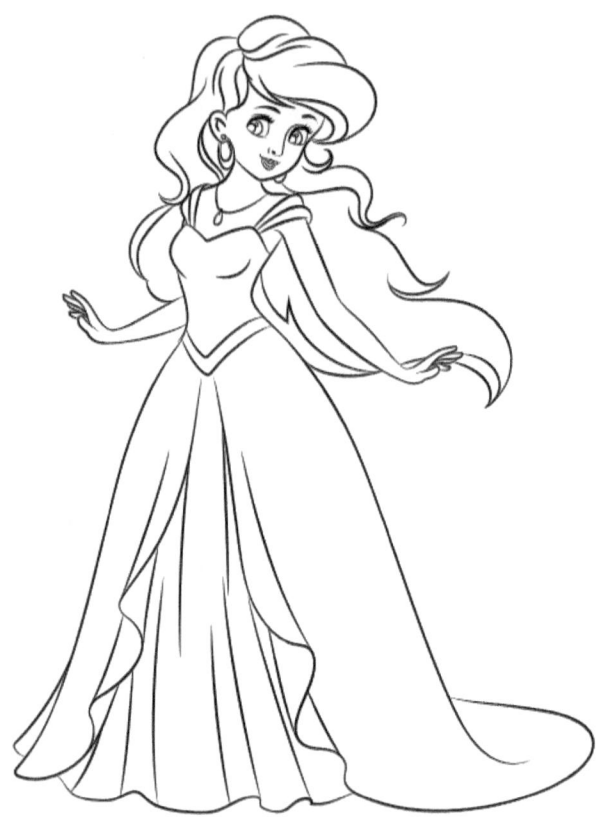

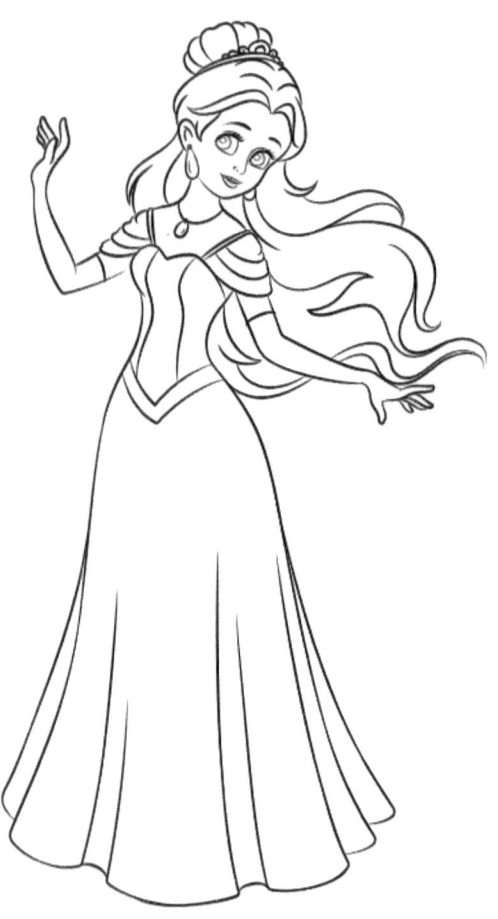

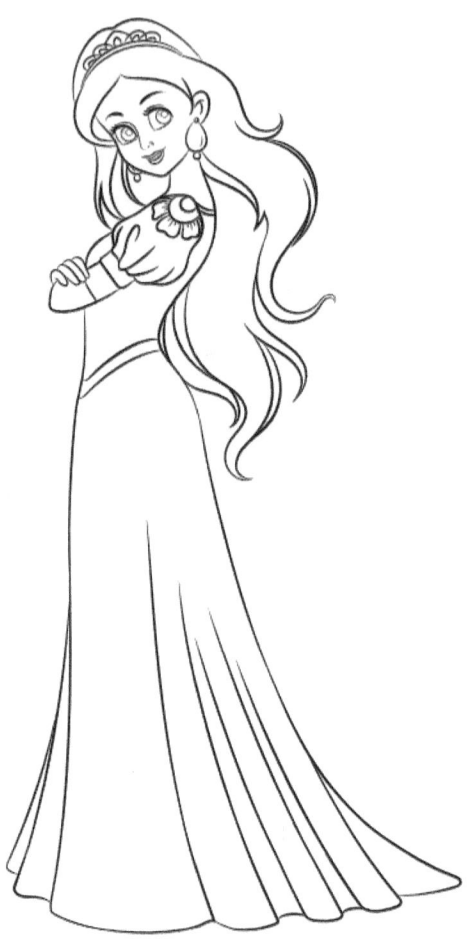

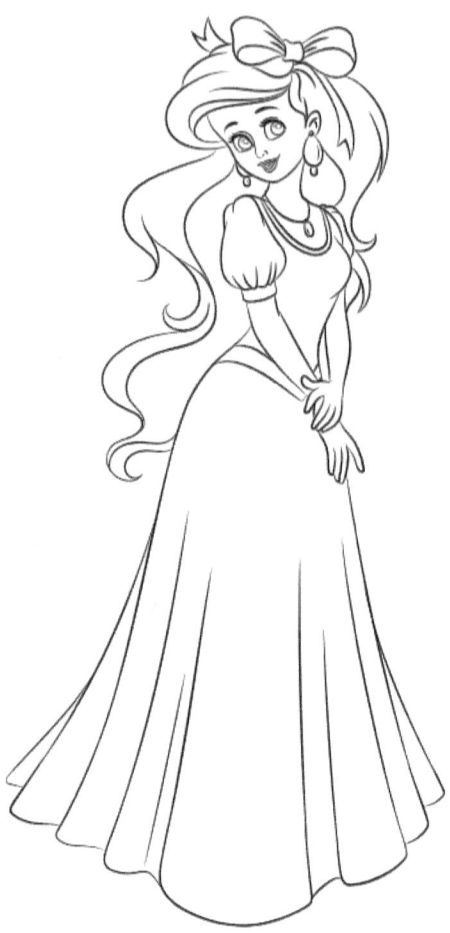

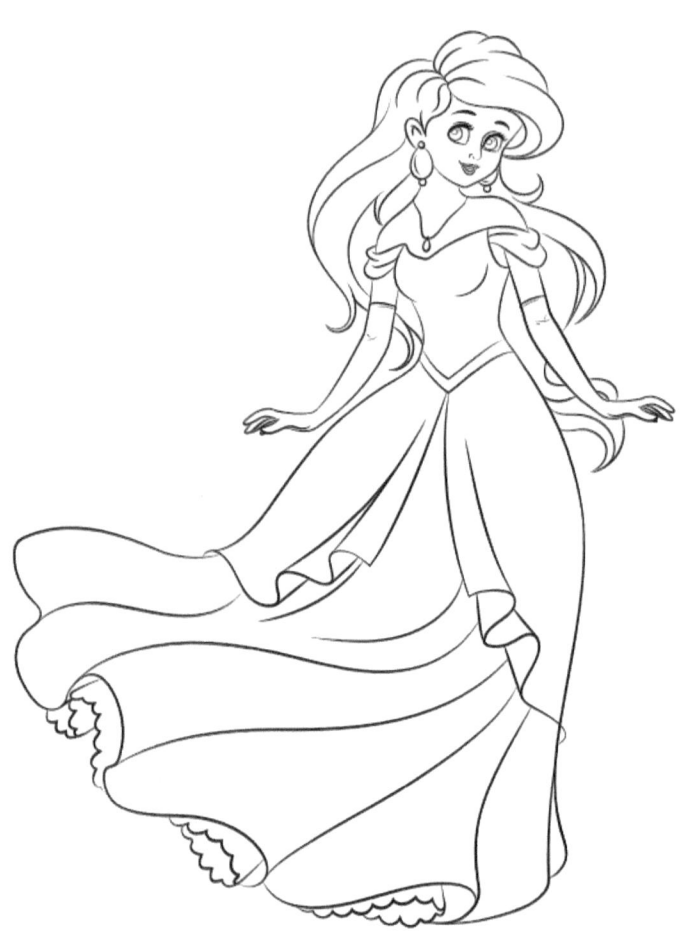

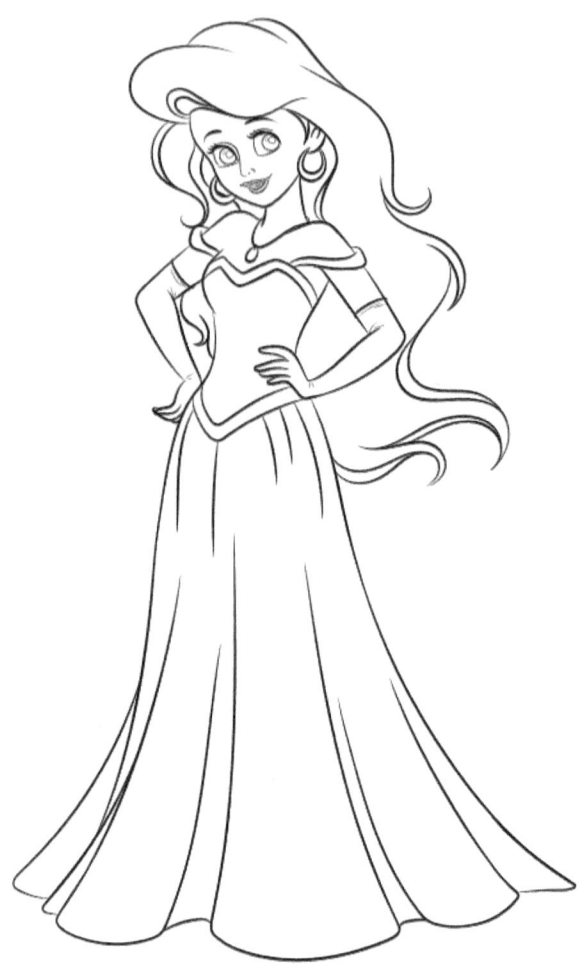

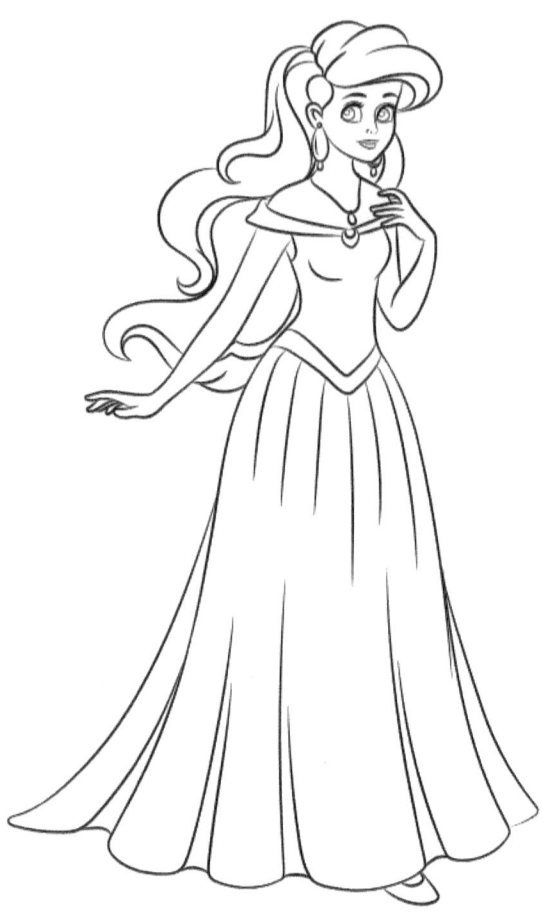

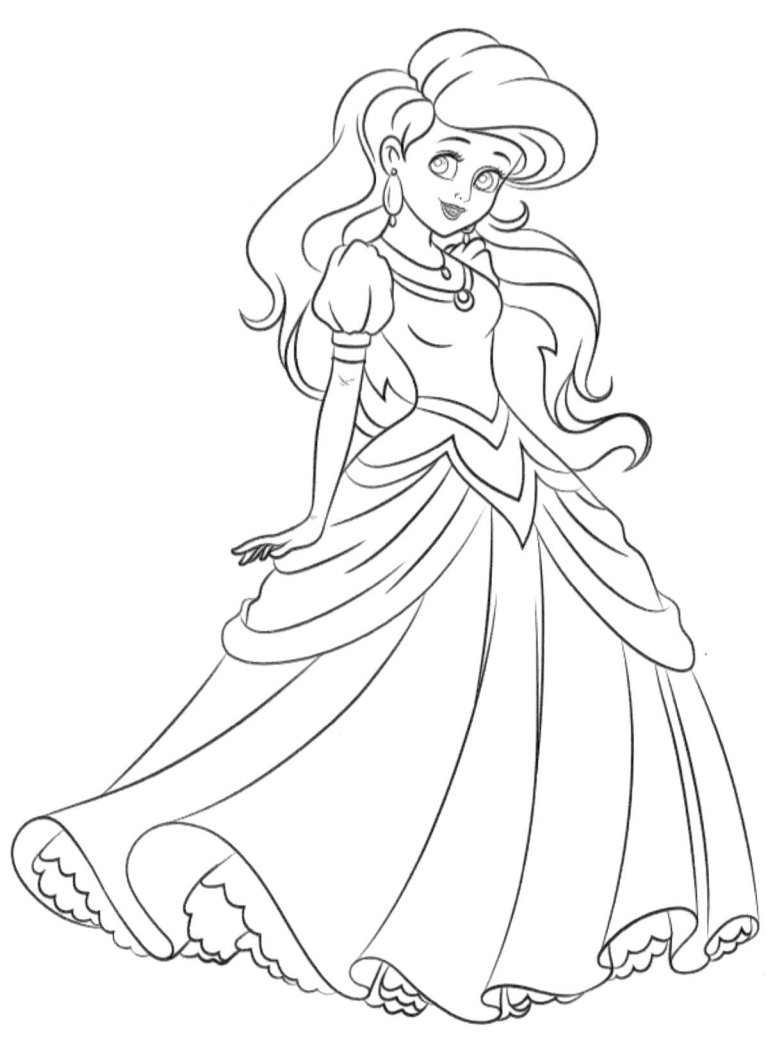

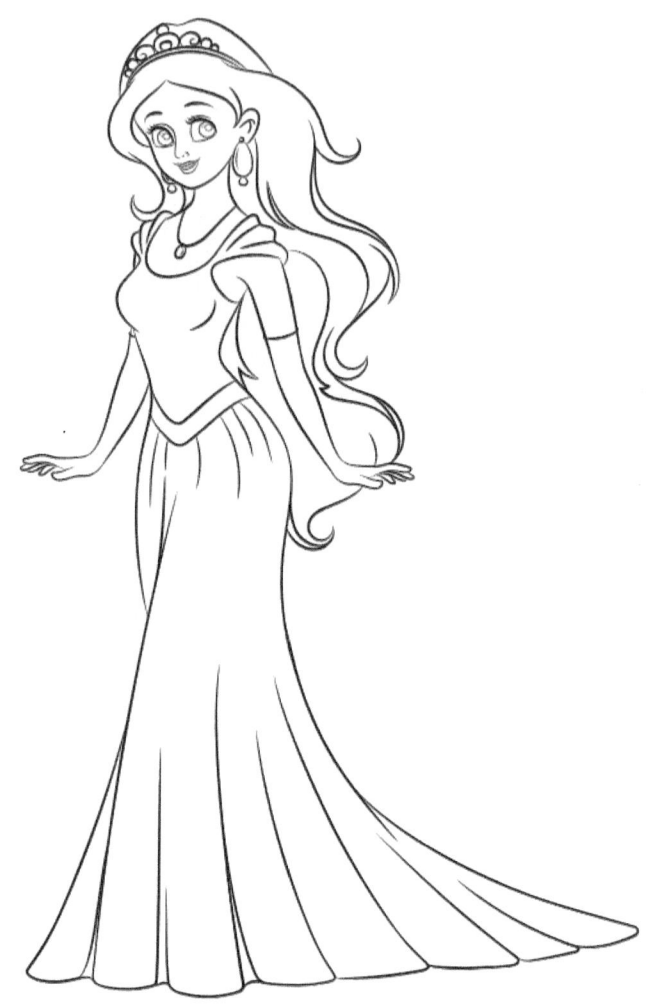

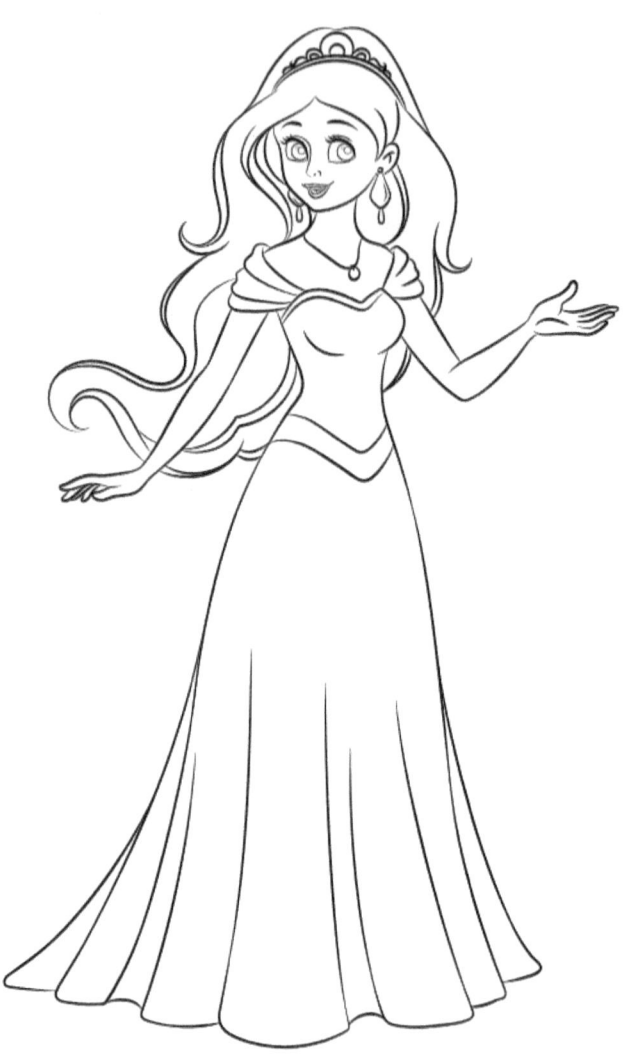

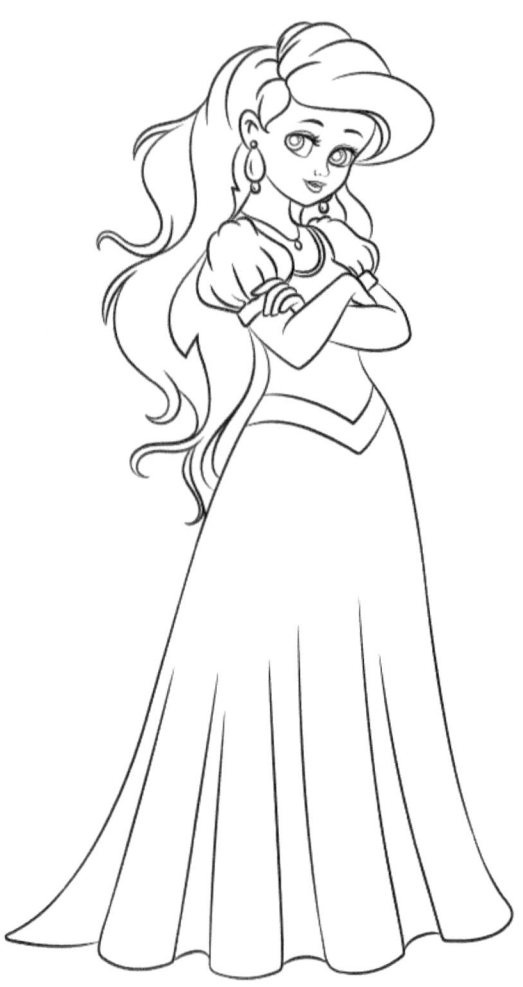

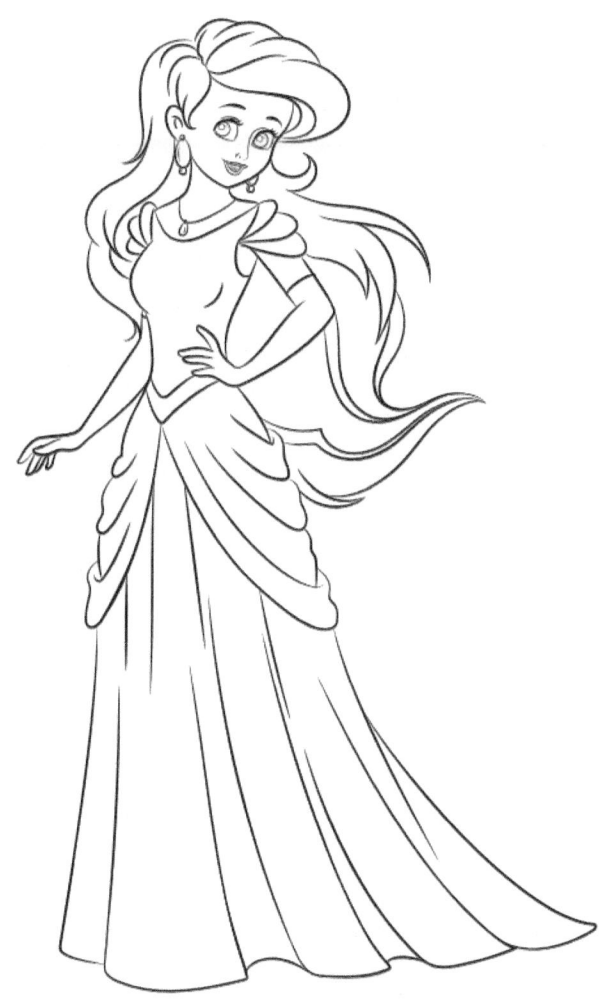

www.ingramcontent.com/pod-product-compliance
Lightning Source LLC
Chambersburg PA
CBHW030955240526
45463CB00016B/2667